W9-BRH-522

RISK TO SUCCEED

RISK TO
SUCCEED

ESSENTIAL LESSONS FOR
DISCOVERING YOUR
UNIQUE TALENTS
AND FINDING SUCCESS

RICKY COHEN

Chairman and CEO The Conway Organization

NEW YORK CHICAGO SAN FRANCISCO
LISBON LONDON MADRID MEXICO CITY MILAN
NEW DELHI SAN JUAN SEOUL SINGAPORE
SYDNEY TORONTO

The *McGraw·Hill* Companies

Copyright © 2013 by Conway Capital, LLC. All rights reserved. Printed in the United States of America. Except as permitted under the United States Copyright Act of 1976, no part of this publication may be reproduced or distributed in any form or by any means, or stored in a database or retrieval system, without the prior written permission of the publisher.

1 2 3 4 5 6 7 8 9 10 DOC/DOC 1 8 7 6 5 4 3 2

ISBN: 978-0-07-180907-8
MHID: 0-07-180907-4

e-book ISBN: 978-0-07-180908-2
e-book MHID: 0-07-180908-5

McGraw-Hill books are available at special quantity discounts to use as premiums and sales promotions or for use in corporate training programs. To contact a representative, please e-mail us at bulksales@mcgraw-hill.com.

Library of Congress Cataloging-in-Publication Data

Cohen, Ricky.
 Risk to succeed : essential lessons for discovering your unique talents and finding success / by Ricky Cohen.
    p. cm.
 ISBN-13: 978-0-07-180907-8 (alk. paper)
 ISBN-10: 0-07-180907-4 (alk. paper)
 1. Success. 2. Self-realization. 3. Conduct of life. I. Title.
 BJ1611.2.C636 2013
 158.1—dc23

                    2012034268

This book is printed on acid-free paper.

Thanks to Blueswitch for their contribution to the interior design of the book.

Design by Lee Fukui and Mauna Eichner

This story about courage, discovery, risk taking, and success is dedicated to the memory of my parents and my brother.

My father, Abe, was a visionary and leader, a southern gentleman, and a perpetual entrepreneur.

My mother, Geri, was a beautiful, regal woman, who committed her life to building the lives of others.

The beneficiaries of their magnificent marriage of 68 years are 6 children, nearly 30 grandchildren, a similar number of great grandchildren, and thousands of men and women in the Sephardic community of Brooklyn, NY.

And to my brother Alfred who died at the age of three. Your purity is our teacher.

Contents

CONTENTS

Acknowledgments

To my student, and friend, Marianna Leybengrub. Thank you for your invaluable insights and the perseverance to bring Bella and Cee to life. May your courage to take risks and your commitment to your dreams guide your life always.

Introduction

"There is no book without an introduction. There is no relationship to the author, his words or ideas. . . ."

We live at a fascinating time.

Intellectual borders are disappearing. Geographic boundaries are blurred. The lines between politics, the business world, and the world of nonprofits are fading as key personalities in each discipline take leadership positions in the others. The local marketplace is global, and stakeholders compete and benefit from talent, brain power, and initiative nurtured at the farthest points on the planet.

The power of the mind has replaced physical strength and is quickly replacing natural resources as the world's currency—the most resilient tool to ensure influence and success.

Smart risk takers have amassed more wealth than nations, and age and experience are revered again, as they were centuries ago.

Opportunities for success and personal fulfillment abound. The constants are courage and the amassing of knowledge. Transparency and integrity are the expected norm, as the "global knowledge economy" peels away the obliqueness from everything and everyone.

There is an unprecedented opportunity for an individual to maximize his career by mastering the age-old principles that have guided human success forever. Whether you're an entrepreneur or an "intra-preneur," (someone looking to maximize his/her success within a traditional organizational structure), the opportunities are great and the *Risk to Succeed* guidelines are invaluable.

Be a student of timeless wisdom and couple that wisdom with consistent, practical application. Risk to Succeed!

The Foundation: Where It Begins

"Your will establishes your reality. A will-driven reality will be even greater than the dream within which it was conceived."

Career success starts with the right foundation.

Axiom #1: Commitment

We live at a time of instant everything.

The immediate accessibility of information and products has great value, yet instant availability and the absence of process may confuse us and give us the sense that all good things are easily and quickly attained.

As is obvious to most—when it comes to the long lasting, defining things in life, there is no instant anything. In fact, the opposite is true. The noteworthy things in life: fulfillment, a good marriage, happy and successful children, and an enriching career, demand an ever growing, creative and intense commitment—oftentimes beyond what we imagine we are capable of giving.

Time, patience, perseverance, more time, new found energy, creativity, and strength, drawn from what we want and hope for, must all be brought to bear to earn life's real trophies.

Commitment is the starting point and the fuel that enables us to build and grow. It is the facilitator of all facilitators.

Make a commitment: If you like what you read on the following pages, work to make it yours.

Axiom #2: "I Come First"

I often hear people say things such as: "I do it all for my children," or "My focus is to reach a certain point in my career where I can retire and commit all of my efforts to the well-being of those around me," and "Isn't that what life's about?"

The answer is no. Life is about putting yourself first. It's about loving you first, caring for you first, and putting your overwhelming efforts into, and your focus on, your well-being and success.

You can't love or care for someone else's "anything" more than your own. And you can't love or care for anyone more than yourself.

When you have a true love of self and focus primarily on your own needs, you will have a greater ability to give to others.

Get comfortable with loving yourself more than you do anybody else—including those you love very much. Care for yourself as the most precious thing you have. Focus on your needs first, and begin to build your days around those needs. This perspective will provide you with much needed strength as you pursue your most right career.

Axiom #3: "The World Was Created for Me"

There is surprising advice presented in the Babylonian Talmud that states, "Each person should wake up in the morning and either think or utter the words: 'The world was created for me.'" Doing so, the Talmudic sages suggest, "affords him/her a different reality than everybody else." How would this work?

You should wake up each morning and think about the vast world in which you live. You should think about the remarkable resources, the talent and ingenuity of the world's many different peoples, the breath of its great inventions and the power of its innovators. When thinking about the marketplace for your product, for example, rather than being concerned about the level of saturation in the market, you should consider that saturation as the platform for what you are about to present. Market conditions and financial and environmental circumstances are the pillars of anyone's product launch or career positioning, put there to enable the person's success. Empowering yourself with this perspective each morning will provide you with a competitive advantage over those around you.

Axiom #4: "I'm Great—Unconditionally"

One of the key perspectives you should own, and an essential perspective you should instill in your children, is the notion of "unconditional greatness." In other words, whether you accomplish heroically or minimally, whether you excel as a student or businessperson or are somewhat average—or even if you fail, you are unconditionally great. "I am great simply because I am."

Man is the pinnacle of the creative process. He has the capacity to reason and to comprehend ideas and concepts that are beyond reason. He has the power to impact the world around him with a simple thought and to change the world with a word or with his silence. He can dream, envision, inspire, and smile. His actions can impact multitudes for generations after the act. He is inherently great.

Greatness doesn't mean perfection, but it does mean an unparalleled and extraordinary existence. Nothing can take away a human being's inherent greatness. It's essential that we own this perspective as we garner the courage to build and grow our careers.

Prologue: A New Life

Would it live?

It was a momentous time in the jungle, almost two years in the making. It was a warm afternoon and the air was filled with excitement and expectation. In the marsh, where the herd of elephants camped, there was anticipation of a new birth. Shefa, the leader of the herd, was expecting her first child!

As the early sun crossed the horizon, the word came to the herd leaders and then to all: A beautiful cow (female elephant) was born, and it appeared healthy. Immediately, the jungle presented its first challenge: Would the cow stand? The laws of the jungle dictate that only those calves that stand within the first hours after birth would live. Word finally came, and to the joy of the herd members, the calf overcame her first challenge—and, with some difficulty, she stood! To Shefa, her newborn was absolutely beautiful! 200 pounds of pure joy! She felt the cow smiling at her as she nursed and warmed it by her side.

Some weeks passed, and the time came for Shefa to choose a name. "Bella," an old and beautiful name, would be given to this new life. "Bella" in ancient jungle scripture means "life's promise."

The laws of the jungle dictate that
only those that stand within the
first hours after birth will live.

RISK TO SUCCEED

PART ONE

JUNGLE WISDOM

REVEAL

CHAPTER I

Bella, the Eight-Year-Old Elephant

Bella was different. Most young elephants were content to move with the herd, keeping close to their older and more experienced relatives. Bella needed to venture out on her own. Each morning she would plot a course a short distance beyond the boundaries of the herd. Each day a little farther than the day before. Each adventure in a slightly different direction.

In truth, Bella's wandering was not only about seeing new places and beings: it was about seeking clues to guide her to her individual path in the jungle. The jungle held great mystery, promise, and truth. It was the most ancient place on earth, the harbinger of life's secrets from the beginning of time. The possibilities offered by the jungle were endless; the options diverse.

Yet many days passed and Bella could not see her own clear choice or direction. With each new sight came new questions. With each new question, Bella's hunger to find her way in the vast and exciting world grew. Although each day began with hope, it ended with disappointment.

Sadly, she wondered, "Who am I? What's my place in the jungle? Is there something life has uniquely designed for me?"

*"What's my place in the jungle?
Is there something life has
uniquely designed for me?"*

CHAPTER II

Cee, the Butterfly

Late one afternoon, a red-and-turquoise speckled butterfly caught Bella's eye. Bella had become accustomed to seeing butterflies on her travels and had even watched some in flight. But this butterfly was different. His movements suggested energy and a mission.

Over time, Bella sensed that this butterfly was bold and unafraid; it landed directly on her trunk, often once, and sometimes several times a day.

One foggy Tuesday morning, approximately forty days into Bella's adventures, the red-and-turquoise speckled butterfly landed on Bella's trunk again—right between her eyes! This time he lingered all morning, taking an interest in Bella's adventure.

After a few hours, the typically soft spoken Bella looked impatiently at her brazen cargo and demanded, "What do you want?"

"Life begins with courage," the butterfly shockingly replied. "The courage to question and the courage to look inside—are the first steps to reveal your unique place in the jungle." And with a colorful flutter of his wings, he was gone.

That day's rain and fog limited Bella's ability to see her new surroundings, so she turned to go home, pondering the butterfly's words as she walked.

"The courage to question and the courage to look inside—are the first steps to reveal your unique place in the jungle."

CHAPTER III

A Curious Partnership

Several days later, Bella spotted the butterfly again. This time, he was on top of the tallest tree in Bella's newly discovered mountain range.

"What's your name?" Bella shouted. "And why do you keep following me?"

"My name is Cee," answered the speckled butterfly. "The jungle harbors great wisdom, ancient wisdom, the wisdom of a thousand generations." Looking directly into Bella's eyes, Cee added, "You have a lot to learn. I want to teach you."

Frustrated, Bella mimed, "You have a lot to teach me? Did you notice you're a butterfly weighing little more than a few ounces? We have nothing in common. What can you teach me?"

"I've traveled this great jungle, flying high over vast mountain ranges, thundering rivers, and towering kapoks," Cee replied, "only to discover that the answers to my questions were not to be found in the mountains I traversed or the river currents that thundered in my ears. Nor were they to be found in the rings of the tallest trees—or in any of the remarkable places I visited."

Looking penetratingly at Bella, Cee revealed, "The answers to my questions were found within me. What you seek lies within you, Bella. Let's reveal it!"

CHAPTER IV

Reveal and Imagine

The following morning Cee was up early, waiting on Bella's trunk. As soon as Bella opened her eyes, Cee proclaimed, "There is no need for your travels today, Bella. There is nothing to be gained by your wandering. The wisdom of the jungle dictates that life's direction comes when you reveal your passion, acknowledge your strengths, and understand your needs.

"Let's begin by exploring the four questions of jungle life. Answering these questions will require a great level of honesty. They may sound simple to you—but in truth, these questions will be the most difficult you've ever considered. The best approach to answering these questions, Bella, is to let the answers come from your gut, not your mind."

Bella, somewhat confused, fairly annoyed, and mildly curious, paused to listen. Seizing the moment, Cee began with the questions.

"Listen carefully, Bella, and memorize each question.

"**Question 1**: If you could choose to pursue any career at all, what would it be?

- "If you didn't have to worry about the herd or what anyone expected of you?

- "If you were guaranteed all the food and protection you would ever need?

- "If you could do anything, go anywhere?

- "If you could venture to a place no elephant has gone before, or do what no elephant may have done until now, what would you choose to do?

"Search inside, Bella. Search within your heart and your in-tuitive sense—and reveal your passion. Once you've done that, Bella, imagine yourself living it! And with that comes the next question.

"**Question 2**: When you imagine yourself living true to your passion, waking up each day pursuing it, and ultimately achieving success—how does that make you feel?

- "Are you inspired, uplifted—and frightened?

- "Do you feel empowered, proud, and energized?

- "Are you afraid you may fail, and at the same time, afraid you may succeed?

"If all of the above are true—you've probably revealed your passion! You have uncovered your unique direction and true expression. If not, go back and try those questions again, with more courage and expansiveness. Stay away from fear and logic! They can interfere.

"Get inside your heart and your gut, Bella!"

Life's most important questions like:
"What is my ideal career?" or "Do I love
her?" must be answered with your gut,
or intuitive sense—that which transcends
your rational and logical mind.

CHAPTER V

Courage

A few days later, Cee returned when it was still dark outside. This time, he jumped from one spot to another on Bella's face, gently forcing her to wake up.

"Cee, what are you doing?"

"Waking up the morning, Bella. Wake up your morning! In the jungle we must bring on the new day and all of its opportunities. We don't wait for the day to come upon us. I gave you homework, and it's due NOW!"

"Homework—*you* gave me homework? You don't think I ask myself those questions every day? I have plenty of ideas, Cee—but they make no sense. You said, 'Go with what's in your heart and your gut!' If I did that, I would be laughed out of the herd and ridiculed by elephants large and small! Be real, Cee—the jungle is a tough and unforgiving place! And by the way, did I mention that butterflies are the most annoying beings in the jungle?"

"Bella, I was once a caterpillar, with no color, no ability to fly, and little ability to see. Could one ever imagine that one day my colors would be brilliant—that I would soar high above this great jungle? My eyes have developed a thousand portals, and I can see quicker and farther than most jungle animals. I was something, became nothing—and then became me! My will established my reality—as can yours! And today, my reality is even greater than my dream!"

Distressed and pleading, Bella answered, "What if I'm just not certain about what I want? What if there are many things I'm interested in pursuing? My dad always felt I was a born educator and should take a teaching position at The Jungle Academy in the marsh. My mom feels I have creative talent and would make a good artist. I've excelled in my painting courses at the Waterfall School for the Arts. Maybe someday I could sell my work at jungle festivals. Dad is right—I can teach others; and Mom is right as well—I'm creative and come up with artistic approaches many wouldn't consider. Cee, I'm torn and confused."

"Okay, Bella, this is a good start," said Cee. "Let's get to work. A friend of mine once gave me a great approach to help figure this out. I call it 'the mirror test.'" And with a quick flutter, Cee produced a little mirror which she had been hiding in her wings. "For this test, describe the two options as you look in the mirror."

Cee watched as Bella stood in front of the mirror describing the possibility of becoming a teacher. She spoke in detail about what she would bring to the teaching profession. She articulated her skills and capabilities, and then she described how a day in her life would look and feel. Cee watched intently—recording in his mind Bella's tone, and body and facial expressions.

And then Bella took a deep breath, did a quick elephant circle, cocked her head, and began to describe her life as an artist. She went on and on about the different styles in which she would paint, the interesting scenery in the jungle she could use as subjects for her work—from the infant orangutans to the sunsets over the southern edge of the marsh, and what a typical day in her artist life would be like.

Cee's eyes never left Bella, and Cee's intensity was unmatched as he focused on each nuance in Bella's manner and every variation in the energy of Bella's voice. Bella's eyes never left the mirror into which she stared.

Once completed, Bella put her head down—drained and tired from the experience. As she lifted her head a few minutes later, tears rolled down her trunk, and she whispered, "The mirror test tells the story so well. Nothing there—no energy, no passion, no anxiety. I guess I failed."

With a warm smile and an expression of compassion in his eyes, Cee whispered, "You were perfect! You naturally projected what you felt inside. There was no passion in your voice or facial expression, no energy in your tone or body language, and no excitement—altogether. In a certain sense, it was painful to watch. Fortunately, we now understand the directions you must NOT consider.

"Tell me, Bella," Cee continued, "What would make you excited to get up in the morning, have you impatient to begin your day? What would raise your elephant spirit if there was no one to please, no demands, no worries? What would you love to do, Bella? Think fun and exciting, new and fresh."

Hesitating, Bella lifted her head slightly, but with a different energy level. In a higher pitched voice, she said, "What I would love to do is crazy—It's silly! No elephant has ever made a living out of doing it. It's unrealistic and illogical." Lowering her head, she continued. "As I've walked from place to place in the jungle, this crazy notion has always been inside of me. It's exciting and real in my mind, but I can't imagine it being real in the jungle."

"Great!" Cee shouted with an excited swirl in the air, "I think we're on to something!"

Bella stood up tall, put down the mirror, stared intensely at Cee for a few minutes, and then said, "I want to open a travel business! I want to organize trips, for those of us who live in the jungle, to the world's great cities!"

Bella continued passionately. "I've seen pictures of New York. I've climbed the Eiffel Tower in my mind. I've dreamed about the great buildings of Rome, the palaces of St. Petersburg, and the skyscrapers of Shanghai. Each day, as I wander a bit beyond our camp, I picture myself arranging for groups of jungle beasts to go beyond the only world they've ever seen—to places they've never dreamed of seeing!

I've memorized travel books, and I'm often up in the middle of the night planning each touring day. I've sketched out fifteen different itineraries! I love to organize, I love animals, and I'm not afraid to work hard. I can barely sleep at night imagining how the lives of the travelers would be enriched as a result of these experiences."

Bella abruptly stopped speaking, lowered her head, looked back into the mirror, and said, "How silly all of this is. To say it's impossible would be an understatement the size of an elephant!"

The mirror is a powerful tool in that it reflects a truth that may be difficult to reveal, one that is felt deep inside of us.

CHAPTER VI

Risk to Succeed

"Spectacular!!!" Cee shouted.

"What?" Bella asked sadly.

"I said Spectacular, Bella! You're on to it!" At this point, Cee became very serious and in a professorial tone, he said, "First, your travel business concept is more than a goal. To some it might appear illogical or unrealistic. To you, it's exciting, energizing, and empowering—exactly what it should be! From the excitement you've displayed, Bella, to the aching to make it happen, it's obvious this interest comes from deep inside of you!" At this point Cee stood, as tall as a butterfly can stand, and said, "It was clear how animated, engaging, and intense you were when describing it! Had you been looking at the mirror, the mirror itself would have been smiling."

Back in his professorial mode, Cee continued. "We're almost there, Bella! Now we have to tie the pieces together—let's focus on the last two jungle life questions—the questions that reveal your strengths and highlight your needs. It's time to identify your natural strengths: the skills that come easily to you and may not come as easily to other elephants. Reveal them all! Tell me about your seemingly unimportant skills and the pronounced ones. Describe the natural abilities that have been noticed by other animals and those that are hidden. List them—Each and every one!"

Cee went on. "You may be a creative thinker—well suited to developing new products or services; or you may be more of a manager—using your understanding of processes and attention to detail to guide others. You may think strategically, with an orientation to the long term—the big picture. Or you may be grounded in the numbers, naturally skilled to ensure that the day to day is functioning and profitable. Listen to me, Bella. The humility for which you elephants are famous has no place here and vanity is not a concern!"

With real annoyance, and a little bit of attitude, Bella retorted, "C'mon Cee, I'm not going to stand here telling you all the 'great' things about me. That may be a butterfly thing—but read my trunk: Elephants don't go there!"

Completely ignoring Bella's protests, Cee spoke with authority. "You've been given certain strengths, natural skills, and capabilities to enable your true interests to be realized. Once we identify your strengths, we can get you on track to do exactly what you have the potential to do. List them now please, Bella!"

Two hours later (elephants are known to be very stubborn at times), Bella fessed up to a list of twenty-two strengths, the highlights of which were the following:

- Creative

- Detail-oriented

- Good management skills

- Enthusiastic team builder

- Follow-up oriented

"So far, so good," Cee thought. "Her strengths speak well to turning her dream into reality; but to establish a clear direction, we need more."

Cee understood that Bella was beginning to get tired— but there was more to do. The last piece—the understanding of Bella's needs—would wrap together all that was put forth so far. With an understanding of Bella's needs, a conclusion could be reached and a new direction established.

Taking on his professorial tone again, Cee said: "At this point, Bella, you must delve a little deeper and identify your needs. You must listen to the voices inside of you that know you well and describe the environment that works best for you. Do you prefer working up front with other animals, for example? Or are you more comfortable being behind the scenes? Would it be more natural for you to be a back-office manager or a field elephant? Are there certain situations you will avoid at all costs and others you look forward to attempting?"

Several hours later (butterflies are known to be very patient at times), Bella and Cee were able to get a clear understanding of Bella's needs—the environment that would work best for this up-and-coming entrepreneur.

Bella admitted to being shy—more comfortable in smaller groups. Although she could clearly imagine herself arranging all of the details of a complex animal trip abroad, she couldn't imagine actually leading the trip. Bella's needs revealed that she was better suited for the planning side of the travel business than the guiding side—that she would be more successful behind the scenes, in a management role, than as a field animal.

"I'm satisfied," Cee said. "Let's call it Bella's Adventures! This career direction reveals your passion, captures your skills and natural strengths, and can work beautifully in a set-up that's comfortable for you.

"Bella's Adventures—it'll rock the jungle!"

Interests + Skills + Needs = Career Success

❧ PART TWO ❧

JUNGLE WISDOM

RISK TO SUCCEED

CHAPTER VII

See and Know

It was one week later, and Bella stopped taking her walks beyond the perimeter of the herd and was hanging around all day, melancholy and defeated. She couldn't even find Cee. A few more days passed until Bella stumbled upon Cee, who was sitting on a large yellow flower soaking up the sun.

"You look terrible, Bella!" Cee chided. "In all my time in the jungle, I don't think I've ever seen a lousier looking elephant!"

With a little bit of anger and a lot of despair, Bella shouted, "Was this all a very bad joke? When was the last time you saw a flock of geese at the Statue of Liberty or a monkey purchasing a ticket to visit Buckingham Palace? What was I thinking? Why did you encourage me?" Bella cried.

After a long period of silence, Cee looked up and commanded, "Stand up on your hind legs, Bella."

"What?" retorted a surprised Bella.

"Hind legs, Bella, you're looking at your front legs." Bella became silent and did as she was told. Anxiously watching Bella, Cee proclaimed, "Not bad. Now stretch your front legs and reach as high as you can. Attempt to touch the top branch of that tree in front of you. Reach farther, farther. Higher, higher. Stretch and reach. Higher! Higher! Keep reaching. Push! C'mon, Bella, push hard, feel some pain, reach higher. C'mon reach higher! Almost, Bella, a little more—push, Bella!"

With an effort on a level never before attempted by Bella, she stood on her hind legs, with her front legs lifted almost to the level of Cee's branch.

"How does it feel, Bella?" Cee demanded.

"It feels good." let out Bella, surprised.

"Stay up there and keep stretching forward," Cee softly demanded. "Stretching your muscles and reaching towards the sky rejuvenates your body and allows you to touch something well beyond your normal reach.

"Now understand this—reaching, intellectually and emotionally, stretching your mind and your imagination, allows you to see and understand things that you've never envisioned before. As you stretch, you become invigorated by the possibility of grasping a place you've never imagined possible. You embrace the essential, life-giving practice of risk taking.

"Know and remember, Bella, that risk taking is every creature's oxygen—regardless of the place in the jungle he occupies. It's the facilitator of the will and the champion of the imagination. Taking risks enables life's journeys and possibilities. You must risk to succeed, Bella! You must risk to succeed! This is the way of the jungle. It always has been this way and always will be this way.

"Let me warn you, Bella. At times you will be afraid to a point of crying. Fairly often, you will doubt all that you had begun to do and be angry at those who encouraged you in this direction. When this happens, don't get discouraged, dear Bella! Know that you are on the right course and that you have begun to build your life. Know that you have begun to stand taller and stronger, expressing your uniqueness among the animals of the jungle. If you fail, if you can't reach or stretch—if you can't create the tension, fear, and anxiety of growth in your life—you will shut the door to the best opportunities of your unique life. And you will never reach your full elephant potential."

Barely taking a breath, Cee continued. "Many beings spend their lifetimes in jungles all over this planet having never truly succeeded, having never ventured beyond themselves to become themselves." At this point, Cee moved to the branch of an old pine tree and continued in a very slow and unusually deliberate tone. "Some jungle creatures believe in a concept called 'Hell.' They believe that at the end of a creature's lifetime, its essence goes to a place with fire, brimstone, and all kinds of things that cause it suffering for the things it did wrong in its life. The creature's essence is

forced to stay there for a while, until it has suffered suffi-
ciently for all of its wrongdoing, and then it moves on to a
place called 'Heaven,' where it is rewarded for all its good
and right deeds.

"In The Butterfly Scroll, we have a different understanding of what happens after a creature's time in the jungle is over. We believe that there is a special place where the
essence of a creature is sent, but that special place has no fire
and causes no harm. Butterflies believe, when an essence
leaves the creature's body, it stands alone in a vast, seemingly
endless valley with two rivers flowing through it. Reflected
on the water's surface, closer to where the essence stands,
are hundreds of pictures, one following after the other,
depicting the life the butterfly led. From the early years,
through its final days, each of a creature's key statements,
decisions, and events are highlighted in full view on the surface of the water. Reflected on the second body of water is
the life that creature had the skills, talent, and potential to
live. Its possibilities, opportunities, and the overall fulfillment it could have experienced dance on the surface of that
river. As the water flows downstream, each of the life mile-
stones that might have been become brighter and brighter.
All of what might have been achieved towers above the water, and the joy that would have been is felt by the observing soul."

And now Cee lowered his voice and, staring straight in
Bella's eyes, continued. "The pain felt at that point is the
realization of what the being's life was versus what it could

have been. The suffering felt is the result of watching, over and over, what the creature had the potential, skills, and opportunity to do—but never did. Those things that held it back—fear, lethargy, or a lack of belief in itself and in life—form a dark cloud around the observing soul.

"True hell is about watching what was—versus what could have been—with no ability to change it."

Straightening up, Cee proclaimed, "If it were me, I'd take the fire and brimstone!" And with a love and intensity Bella had not seen before, Cee continued. "Bella, we want to do everything we can so that what is reflected on each of the waters is overwhelmingly the same!"

Cee gave Bella a smile and a verbal pat on the back as he concluded, "Get out there and get started! Oh, and by the way, you can put your legs down now, Bella."

It's not about fire and brimstone.
It's about living the life a
creature was endowed to live.

CHAPTER VIII

Execute

"Great speech, Cee," Bella retorted seemingly unmoved. "What exactly should I do?"

"Achieving seemingly unrealistic goals starts with a reality-based plan," Cee answered.

Reclaiming his professorial tone, Cee elaborated. "First, put together a 'timeline to success.' A timeline to success is a time and action plan that lists, in detail, your immediate and your three-, six-, and nine-month goals and what you must do to achieve them.

"Next, connect with a 'success partner.' A success partner is a creature who understands you well. He or she will be your mentor and your conscience, and will help you move forward. She knows you well enough to anticipate your fears and challenges, while also rebuking you when necessary. He will help you clearly articulate your strengths and your vision. A success partner is essential. You're one lucky elephant, Bella—because you've got me!

"The next step is to begin living it. Dedicate at least five hours a week to living what you want most—even if you haven't yet figured out how to make it a financial success.

"Now, get moving!"

As Bella replied, an attitude in her voice meekly crept in. "This all sounds nice, Cee, but my Dad stopped by last night. I have to begin to earn my keep in the jungle! He told me that I have to get a full-time job. He feels strongly that I have responsibilities that have been largely left unmet. I don't have the luxury, at this point, to experiment for five hours a week with something I would like to do . . ."

"I think you do," Cee said, interrupting Bella. "Everybody has five hours a week. It goes like this: Get a full-time job, for forty hours a week, if necessary, but look at the rest of your waking hours very carefully so that you can carve out a minimum of five hours to do what you love to do. You'll find that your time doing what you want most will turbo-charge your day job with energy and creativity. You'll perform better at the job you need to be doing when you're engaged, even in a limited way, in what you most want to do!

"Over time, life will reward your courage and perseverance and the balance will shift in the direction of what you were truly built to do. The five enriching hours a week will grow and the forty hours will become less and less. The hours spent doing what you love will ultimately become full time as your efforts are greeted with success!

"Now get moving!"

Small, Reality–Based Steps
+ A Success Buddy
+ A Measurable Time Commitment =
The Realization of "Unrealistic" Goals

CHAPTER IX

The Reality Is Bigger than the Dream

Six months later, a large banner hung on the tree by the campsite of Bella and her family.

BELLA'S ADVENTURES
Jungle Travel Worldwide

Below the banner, an additional sign read:

10% Off for the First Twenty Customers

And below this additional sign were heads—dozens of heads of animals of all kinds. Lions, tigers, bears, coyotes, orangutans, and even a family of giraffes, all lined up as far as the eye could see. All were excited about visiting the destinations of their dreams.

Under the eucalyptus trees, Bella and Cee were busy custom designing each trip for each and every group. And then all the real work began! It started with getting a reservations' person on the phone who understood the Jungalee's language. It continued with convincing him to accept Bella's unique tourists. And then the seemingly impossible task of working out payments in barter (jungle animals have no access to human currency).

What was the correct amount of frog eggs to cover the admission for five to the Eiffel Tower? Could the deer hides provided by the tiger family pay for their nine business-class tickets to San Francisco?

And when all of that was done, the logistical work began. The "Bella's Adventures" team worked through unprecedented logistical issues:

- Seating an elephant comfortably on a Boeing 767 airplane

- Arranging a tour bus that could accommodate a family of giraffes

- Getting a fine restaurant to accept a reservation from the South East Jungle Reptile Union

- And securing a visit to the top of the Empire State Building for a group of wild buffalo with an average weight of one ton

Bella's five hours a week became fifty. Her receptionist and manager, Cee, was exhausted, and they couldn't keep a logistics coordinator for more than a few days. In fact, the reality was bigger than the dream!

Bella never imagined how fulfilled and uplifted she would feel, as she looked back on each exhausting day.

And so it began.

PART THREE

JUNGLE WISDOM

SHED, SHED, SAVE

CHAPTER X

Bumps

For a few months, although exhausted, the small team at Bella's Adventures was doing well. Then things changed. Somehow it seemed as if the entire world turned upside down and everyone had gone mad!

The World Travel Association scheduled a conference in Geneva, Switzerland, to adopt a binding resolution against animal travel.

Weight restrictions were instituted for passengers on the larger, international airlines.

The Council of Fine Restaurants began circulating a memorandum to change the entity's bylaws to include rigorous etiquette requirements in their restaurants, one of which was that a customer must demonstrate the ability to walk into a restaurant on two legs and eat with two hands.

The environmentalist group, "Jungles, the Final Frontier," had its 237 branches begin circulating petitions stating that buses transporting the jungle animals to the airport posed a threat to the environment.

All at once, the dreamlike reality at Bella's Adventures was gone.

Bella's clientele, the animals of the jungle, were frightened and felt discriminated against. Most cancelled their plans. Others decided to postpone their trips—indefinitely. Everywhere Bella turned, there was another seemingly insurmountable challenge. And each day added to the previous day's difficulties.

"How could I not have anticipated these problems?" Bella demanded. "Why wasn't I more careful? Why didn't I move more slowly? How am I going to face my customers who expect me to deliver what I've promised?" she wondered.

Bella closed the office to the public and mounted a new sign, the first since the ones that she hung on the day she opened for business.

It read:

BELLA'S ADVENTURES
Closed for Travel Holiday

Bella sat in the office alone. The phone didn't ring, and the computers were turned off. She wouldn't move. She simply sat at her desk, day after day, tearful and brokenhearted.

Late one afternoon there was a knock on her door. Bella thought, "Best if I ignore it so they think the office is empty." The knock persisted for several minutes, and then a soft voice began to call her name.

Bella recognized the voice. It was her mom, Shefa. Yet Bella remained still and silent, feeling like she couldn't face her mom at this heartbreaking time. She couldn't bear to see her mom's reaction to learning that Bella's business was finished, that there was nothing left. "If only I had anticipated these issues," Bella repeated to herself, over and over, with a great sense of guilt and self-doubt.

Shefa refused to leave. She had not seen her daughter in days, and she had heard the whispers of the chirping birds about how Bella was secluding herself in her office, refusing to speak to anyone.

"Bella, it's cold out here and it's getting dark, but I will not leave until you let me in! Please, Bella, I must see you," Shefa pleaded.

Bella understood it was getting dark and would soon become dangerous for her mom to be alone outside in the jungle night, so she grudgingly opened the door. When her mother entered the room, Bella collapsed onto Shefa's trunk and began to sob.

CHAPTER XI

Shed, Shed, Save

When Bella was young, Shefa would tell her stories every night. They were uplifting and beautiful stories, which sometimes ended with a song. As Shefa held her daughter that evening, she began to tell Bella a story she had never told her before.

"There was a pretty, young elephant," Shefa began, "who fell in love with a handsome, male elephant many years older than her. It was the kind of romance you rarely hear about in the jungle—a beautiful pair, deeply in love, with the support and enthusiasm of their family and friends.

"Then one day, without warning, it all changed. The male elephant was gone, without a word, without a good-bye. Days went by, and he didn't return to the herd. Months went by, and word got back that he had found another cow."

At this point Shefa stopped telling the story and began to cry softly, barely noticeable tears running down her trunk. "I couldn't understand why he left me. I could only blame myself. I considered it my failure. For months, I carried my pain and the self-blame, not allowing myself to let it go. For months, I played the experience over and over again in my head, with a great sense of guilt and self-judgment.

"And then there was a point when I took my life back! After scores of lost days and sleepless nights, I came up with a plan to move my life forward based on the direction given to me by one of the elders of the jungle. I will share with you, Bella, what was told to me a long time ago. It's called 'The Jungle Code of Liberation.' Its preamble starts something like this: 'We're quick to forgive strangers, less quick to forgive those we love, and we have the most difficult time forgiving ourselves. Guilt is a destructive emotion.'

"The Code advises that guilt must be removed as quickly as it comes. When you fail, forgive yourself quickly—as you would forgive a well-intentioned stranger— because you are no less deserving than he. Shed the pain and the guilt attached to the failure; shed the experience from your mind, and save the lessons to use in building something greater than before.

"Shed, Shed, Save!

"The Code is long, and you may learn it over time, but it closes with words that enable you to understand all of the insights provided within it:

'Stumbling: A gift.
Pain: Life's teacher.
Fail in front of all whom you love—and become free.

Stumbling: A gift.

Pain: Life's teacher.

Fail in front of all whom you love—and become free.'"

Bella wondered, "A gift? Life's teacher? Why would anyone want a public failure?"

As if she were inside Bella's thoughts, her mother answered, "Dearest Bella, failure is a gift; its lessons are priceless. A public failure is life's cherished gift, in that it frees you to never be afraid again! A public failure forces you to stand unprotected, in front of every creature about whom you care, and to understand once and forever that the only thing to be afraid of in life is the failure to try, not the failure of trying.

"A public failure is life's liberator!"

And as her mom left, with an intense hug and words of love, Bella whispered to herself, "Stumbling is a gift. Pain is life's teacher. I have been blessed with a failure in front of the eyes of all whom I love. Stumbling is a gift. Pain is life's teacher. I have been blessed with a failure in front of the eyes of all whom I love . . .

"I am free." And she smiled through her tears.

Bella barely slept that night. She was anxious to begin a new day and to challenge all that had challenged her. As the morning sun began to break through, she summoned a level of strength she had never identified as hers and demanded a phone meeting with the chairman and CEO of The World Travel Association. If he would not take the phone, Bella suggested to a harried receptionist, she would bring 100,000 beasts, from jungles on three different continents, to march on the WTA offices in Geneva. "Animals from the canine and feline species have been traveling for decades—as have beasts of burden!" Bella proclaimed. "Any attempt to restrict the travel of jungle beasts will be met with fierce opposition."

The next step was the airlines. Here Bella tapped into the skills of her father, a seasoned politician and diplomat, to negotiate a fee structure that would compensate the airlines for any additional costs incurred due to the level of care required of the unique jungle passengers. The initial response of "This will never happen!" was followed by a complex but fair deal for all of the stakeholders: the travelers, the airlines, and the travel agency.

The issue with The Council of Fine Restaurants would prove more complex. "How do I convince the finest restaurants in the world's greatest cities that the dining experience of their guests would be enhanced by allowing jungle animals access?" For this, Bella hired a well-known public relations firm with offices in New York, London, and Paris. After a 60-day development period, they agreed to launch a campaign titled, "Animals are Man's Best Friends." Press conferences were held with key jungle personalities and animal lovers in capital cities in the United States and Europe. Within a year, the restaurants were reaching out to Bella's Adventures to secure reservations for small groups of jungle travelers.

The environmental campaign posed a different set of challenges and required its unique response. In this case, Bella hired a part-time employee to work exclusively with the environmentalists. With the help of a newfound ally at the WTA, a framework of safeguards was developed to ensure that the jungle ecosystem was not compromised by the new levels of traffic. In addition, a jungle safari, the result of a collaborative effort between Bella's Adventures, and Jungles, The Final Frontier, would be held each summer. The safari would be attended by humans and jungle animals, and would focus on the fragility of the jungle habitat.

It took resolve and courage, but within a number of months Bella's Adventures was back! The pent-up demand for travel made business better than ever before.

I wish my children and all of those

about whom I care

a giant, public failure—

as soon as possible.

PART FOUR

JUNGLE WISDOM

SURVIVAL IN THE JUNGLE

CHAPTER XII

Learn to Learn

"Bella, we need a day off," Cee proclaimed early one morning.

"What are you talking about, Cee? Things have begun to clear up and we've got tons of work to get done."

"Correct," Cee answered undeterred. "We're closing shop for the day for some off-site training. I call it 'Workshop in the Wild.'"

With that, Cee led a grudging Bella out of her office and toward the direction of Bella's home.

"Where are we going, Cee?" protested Bella. "I've had enough of your mysteries. I've also got a lot on my mind."

"We're going to spend a little time in your room," Cee suggested with a hint of suspense.

"Where?" Bella tried to insist convincingly.

A minute or so later, Cee proclaimed with a smile, "We're here! Great room, Bella," Cee observed, "but something's missing. Any other areas in the cave you call yours?"

"I told you, Cee, I'm not interested in your riddles to-day."

"The most important element in this room is missing. What do you think is missing, Bella?"

"Did you ever see an elephant run away from a butter-fly? Cut me a break, Cee."

"Listen, Bella, the last period in your career taught you to deal with failure and treat it as life's enabler and libera-tor. Now it's time for you to learn to anticipate bumps and shifts in the direction of things. It's time for you to become a leader of change. In other words, Bella, where are your books?"

"Talk to my trunk, Cee."

"Life in the jungle will often put an entrepreneur in situations that are unexpected. Elephants have good memories, but must learn to anticipate, or 'to expect the unexpected,' as butterflies are prone to say. The only way for you to do that, Bella, is to constantly learn and grow through new ideas. You must read or study things each day that expand and challenge all that you know. You must stay fresh and curious, unafraid to revisit or reject something you've always assumed to be true. To be one step ahead of change and ultimately become a leader of change is about learning to learn and becoming a perpetual student."

Sensing that Bella was listening, Cee continued. "It goes like this: First, you should read or study something new every day. You should read things related to what you do for a liv-ing, but more important than that, you've got to read things that have nothing to do with what you do for a living! Read about architecture and education. Become familiar with world events and chemistry. Relearn the mathematics and language arts you were taught in high school. Learn whatever you enjoy learning—as long as you break a mental sweat, challenging yourself each day with new information."

"Are you finished, Cee? Can we get back to work?" Bella challenged.

As if he hadn't heard Bella, Cee continued. "Next, you've got to establish a set time for that learning. It can be as little as fifteen minutes a day, but it must be focused and it must be consistent. You can't skip it! And if there's an emergency, you make up the learning time. What do you think, Bella?"

"It won't happen, Cee. I've got a serious business. And I love what I do. I think about 'Bella's Adventures' all the time. You want me to leave all of that and study philosophy?"

"I didn't think you were the philosophical type, Bella, but that works."

"Let's get back to our customers," Bella said with a sigh.

"The best way to make it work, Bella, is to hook up with a 'study buddy;' someone equally committed to new growth and knowledge, who will either study each day's new material with you or will challenge your understanding of things as you challenge his or hers."

"You want me to study philosophy with a chimpanzee?"

"Again, if we're talking about ongoing learning, I like the cat family more than the ape family, but yes, that's correct.

There's one more piece, Bella," Cee continued. You should fill your room with books (electronic readers hadn't hit the jungle yet). Each month, get a new book and add it to your library. Whether you read the entire book that month or just a few pages; a growing library is essential for a perpetual student. Got it, Bella?

"When you learn something new each day, you'll be open, wondrous, and curious. You'll thrive in the travel business or any business you may undertake over the long term. You'll be where you need to be when a curve ball comes your way. Knowledge is the only thing that is eternal in the universal order of beings. Once earned, it is yours, forever. It will frame each of your days and provide you with a distinctive edge as a business leader and entrepreneur."

Surprisingly, Bella responded, "Got it, Cee. I can think about the library on the way back to the office. And monkeys are brighter than you think!"

A person can only be a successful entrepreneur if he or she is a perpetual student.

Smart is the new rich.

CHAPTER XIII

Journey into the Forbidden Forest

At the outer limits of the jungle lay a dark and foreboding place. It never appeared on the jungle maps designed by the coyotes who typically served as scouts for the herds. The jungle beasts never ventured there in that it was rumored to be a place of great challenges from which many failed to return. It was rumored that the challenges weren't physical in nature, but rather were challenges of the mind.

Early one morning, before the sun rose, Cee made his way to Bella's nightly resting place and began to whisper to her that it was time to wake up for a special journey. Bella, like most elephants, cherished her rest. As a working elephant she counted on every moment of sleep to grant her the clarity of mind to maximize her daily study session and to then run her company.

This morning, Cee softly demanded that Bella rise and begin her day with a journey to a place she'd never seen. Bella was too tired to protest, so with a bit of grunting and some feeble complaining, she followed Cee beyond the boundaries of the herd and beyond those boundaries that even she had explored in her earlier travels.

As they walked, Cee spoke about concepts Bella had never heard before. He spoke about a collective consciousness where all of the universe's knowledge was gathered and shared. And he spoke about the ability to harvest some of that collective knowledge in order to lead and to succeed.

And then they arrived. It was still very dark, but in the distance they were able to see the movements of different figures—some small and others incredibly large; none clearly discernible.

When they reached a point where the darkness seemed most pronounced, Cee asked Bella to sit down and close her eyes.

Some time passed, and he asked Bella to think about the three most pressing issues she faced as a business elephant, and the most urgent concerns she had as a single female. Cee suggested that Bella think about nothing else and that she allow the early morning calm and the uniqueness of the place to inspire her.

A number of minutes went by, and Cee handed Bella a large leaf, an ostrich feather, and dye from the wild berries in the area. He then asked her to record everything that came to her mind. Cee implored Bella that she neither edit nor assess—just record.

As the morning light began to shine over the horizon, Bella began to write. She filled the first leaf and asked for a second, and then a third and a fourth. In total, she filled six large leaves with her thoughts focused around the issues that most concerned her at that time.

When Cee sensed that Bella's writing was complete, he collected the leaves and suggested that they begin their way back to the marsh. As they walked, Cee sat on Bella's back and began to explain. He called their little exercise "The Morning Harvest" and described how his jungle ancestors had the practice of beginning each day not with a rush to address the day's demands, but rather with a period of time spent thinking about life's most pressing issues and recording what came to mind. Cee explained that at night there is a "consciousness convention" in the universe which provides for the sharing of ideas and the unlocking of insights. He suggested this is one of the powerful tools that living beings are given to help them understand their world and master its demands.

"The forbidden forest is a place that immediately opens one's mind," Cee said, "but a quiet corner would, over time, do the same thing." He suggested that if the insights weren't immediately recorded, they would be lost.

Of all that Cee had taught Bella, this was certainly the most strange and most difficult to understand. But by now

Bella deeply trusted Cee and had faith in his wisdom. Once they returned home, Bella read what she had written—ideas and insights she couldn't possibly have written even a short time later!

From that day forward, Bella began each day by dedicating ten minutes to reflect on the key issues in her life and to write down each and every thought that came to mind. Some days she wrote several pages, others a line or two, and some days she wrote nothing at all; but everything she wrote was insightful and valuable, adding immeasurably to the knowledge and insights she used to grow and succeed.

List it or lose it. The first moments of the morning offer unparalleled insights to life's most daunting challenges and most exciting opportunities.

CHAPTER XIV

Jungle Justice

Six months passed, and things were going great at Bella's Adventures. Bella had a bright study buddy, was putting in almost forty-five minutes of learning each day, and had collected almost twenty books. She spent several minutes each morning harvesting the insights afforded to her during the night, producing her written notes that were invaluable.

But the happiness she had felt and the excitement that would pump her up each day was waning. And that confused her. Bella was doing what she loved most and at the same time she was growing intellectually, both in her capacity to understand and reason complex issues and in her accumulation of knowledge. She was becoming the most affluent and accomplished female in the herd, but she felt unfulfilled.

"Maybe I am glum because of Cee's absence," Bella thought. Cee hadn't been around the jungle for a while. He was leading a group of rhinos through a four-week adventure in the Sub-Saharan Desert.

One morning, Bella's dad stopped by the office and noticed his daughter seemed tired and sad.

"Hi, Bella, want to do an early lunch?" (Even elephants do that kind of thing sometimes.)

"I can't, Dad. I have a group of bald eagles leaving for a vacation in Vail, Colorado, tomorrow and I still haven't gotten the ski rentals worked out."

"You know, Bella, my grandfather taught me something important a long time ago. He told me that an elephant needs a number of different things to make her happy."

Out of respect for her father, Bella put down her ledger and looked up.

"A career is one of them," Elie continued. "You're a superstar in that sense. There isn't, nor has there been, an animal in the jungle who has achieved what you have. In addition to your extraordinary career success, your level of knowledge is recognized as well. There isn't an animal that doesn't acknowledge how well read you are.

"You've inspired every jungle being from the tadpoles to the storks. My dear, Bella, even some of the insects are starting to take notice! But there's something missing in your life. An elephant's soul has different parts which have different needs. We have a need to do something practical that is creative and speaks directly to what we love and can do well; that's the career component of our lives. We have a need to keep growing intellectually, so we remain stimulated and stimulating, open and curious, ready for change and champions of change.

"Yet there is another side to us that is no less impactful to who we are and our ability to succeed. And that is, doing for others. A creature must reach out, find other creatures in pain, and do something to help remove that pain. He or she must secure another piece of the happiness life offers by doing a greater good."

Bella thought she must be hearing things. "How could her father, who was so astute, so worldly—be so off track? How could he be talking about this kind of thing at this point?"

With great care and sweetness, Bella answered, "Daddy, I love you with all of the love an elephant can feel, and I have the greatest respect for how you've dedicated your life to guiding our herd. Without your direction we would be lost! But Daddy, you're a herd councilman—I'm a business elephant."

"I understand where you're going, Bella," Elie interrupted. "Allow me to continue. "A successful herd official, if that is what he does professionally, must look for additional ways to help others outside of what he gets compensated to do. I take a few hours every Sunday morning, when I'm off from my herd responsibilities, to teach some of the sea lions' pups down by the river. I love animals and I love science, so this gives me an opportunity to help those who are doing poorly in their studies.

"You know, Bella, I enjoy what I do for a career and I believe I do it well, but the fulfillment I feel when a sea lion pup smiles because she's beginning to understand something that had challenged her makes me very happy. It fills me inside in a way nothing else can."

"Daddy, I'm a single cow with a growing business. I study every day—without fail. I help jungle animals every day when I plan an adventure they otherwise wouldn't have taken. I'm tired, Daddy, and I can't imagine doing anything more right now."

"Tell me, Bella," her father persisted, "What reality of jungle life makes you sad or troubles you?"

"Daddy I'm barely nine years old," Bella protested. "I don't think about these things!"

"Well, think for a minute, Bella. If you could remove a piece of sadness from an animal's life, where would you focus?"

Anxious to end the conversation, but aware of the respect due to her father, Bella offered, "I feel sad when I see a creative leopard, or a talented gorilla, who could be doing so much with his or her life, but was never guided on how to do it."

Once those words left her lips, Bella inspired herself to continue. "You know, Daddy, the guidance Cee gave me is the most important gift I have ever been given, other than the love you and Mom gave me. I would be happy to share that with some of the young coyotes, for example, who get into trouble as a result of their boredom. I would be thrilled to show them how much life really offers and how each could do something unique for himself."

"So there you are, Bella. It's essential in life to find a way to give to others, and the one who benefits most is the giver, not the recipient. You should be involved in something outside of your career that will enrich the lives of others by removing pain or helping them grow. And you should choose that effort based on what makes you happy."

"I could do it, Daddy!" Bella proclaimed joyfully. "I could put together a short course on finding the perfect career. I'm sure Cee would help me. We could go from species to species and begin to build a generation of jungle animals that will engage the world in ways never dreamed of before. How fantastic would that be? And the animals who succeed in this generation could offer the same guidance to those who follow them. We could create an entirely new perspective about jungle living!" Bella nearly shouted.

"Sounds like you may have something there, Bella. Try it for a few months and give it a minimum of an hour a week. Measure how you feel while you're doing it. You should feel excited. You should be having fun. In fact, at times, you should feel like you are benefiting more than the recipients!

"Our ancestors called this 'Jungle Justice.' Helping another is to act justly and righteously. It will empower you and strengthen you. Doing for your fellow creatures will create a different reality for you, a reality that will give you the strength to persevere as you continue to pursue your goals and dreams. By enriching the lives of others, you will grant yourself another dimension of fulfillment—and with that, a greater ability to succeed."

With love and understanding, Elie continued. "If or when that good feeling goes away, take time off and figure out your next expression of giving. The more you give to others, the more you give to yourself!"

And with a warm embrace, Bella's father bid farewell.

Those who are committed to creatures and situations greater than themselves will achieve things greater than themselves.

CHAPTER XV

The School for Animal Excellence

It didn't take long for Bella to get her educational efforts going. Once she mentioned to her customers that she was willing to share the secrets that enabled her to build her business, there was interest from every animal right down to the jungle rats.

Bella was actually visited one day by a group of hornets from the marsh who felt discriminated against. They complained that she hadn't been helping the jungle insects! She agreed to work with the insect community once she got all the kinks out of her animal presentation.

So it was that "The School for Animal Excellence" opened in an old shed in the valley. Each month, Bella would give a series of four Sunday morning classes on how to delve inside, reveal your excellence, deal with failure, become a master of change, and persevere as a result of giving to others. The creativity and direction undertaken by some of her students was remarkable!

Leo the Lion put together his love for sports, his love for animals, and his powerful position in the jungle to provide something never dreamt of before. Leo opened "Fabulous Fours," a school for animal extreme sports. And, wow, what a success it was! In the first three weeks, nearly 300 jungle animals attended training courses, 100 of whom walked or galloped nearly two hours to get there.

Jackie, one of the young female giraffes, began a bird-watching society. Jackie harnessed her fascination with animals that could fly, with the extensive studies she undertook on the different species of winged beings. By the end of the first year, she had organized three, adult bird-watching groups and one pup group!

The student in whom Bella took the most pride was a deer, Stephan, who had been maimed in a jungle accident and came to her program having all but given up on doing anything professionally with his life. Stephan struggled for weeks to identify something for which he had a passion and that could be done in his limited physical state.

Cee took a special liking to Stephan and would give him private counseling, trying to help him identify his key interests and strengths. Cee stressed over and over again that life would not afford him interests and strengths, only then to not allow him the opportunity to use them.

Finally, one morning after Stephan had a tearful exchange with Cee, it all came together for him. Stephan would design and sell jewelry for creatures of the jungle! He had always been creative. He could take small, colored stones, place them on pieces of bark from trees—with different colors and textures, and create various finishes using other stones and leaves.

Within a few months, the jungle was transformed! Elephants had toe rings. Lions were seen wearing large, bright crowns on their heads, with stones set in unusually shaped pieces of bark. Owls could be spotted wearing bandanas sporting small, multicolored gems that glowed at night. Jungle pigs, male and female, began wearing nose rings in fabulous shapes and colors. There was barely a giraffe to be seen who didn't have between two and five necklaces on her neck. Peacocks were spotted wearing high platform shoes with iridescent colored stones attached. And there was even a sighting of a large scorpion with bracelets on each of her arms and legs.

What a success story for Stephan!

And as for Bella, she was happier than she had ever been. She had an excellent career, she was growing in new knowledge and insight as a result of her learning, and now as a result of giving to others, she had fulfilled a part of her being she had never dreamed could be so prominent, its power so great in shaping how she felt each day.

CHAPTER XVI

The End of a Chapter

Bella and Cee had a wonderful summer. They arranged scores of trips to new and unchartered parts of the world and successfully negotiated a franchise arrangement with groups interested in replicating Bella's Adventure's with fish and insects. What an extraordinary time it was!

One day, as they prepared to leave the office, Cee turned to Bella and said, "It's time for me to say goodbye. What we shared is ours forever, but I must begin the next stage of my life—and you must begin yours."

"C'mon, Cee, I thought we were done with your crazy ideas. We're a team! We're partners forever!"

"There are two books on your desk, Bella. One book is a collection of eight parables given to me by the wisest butterfly I ever knew: my father. It is now time for you to have it. These parables will enrich your life. Read them on every birthday and anniversary. Each time you read them, you will discover greater depths of life's understanding in their words.

"The second book is a collection of lessons I've learned throughout my life. I can think of no jungle animal with whom I would leave them other than you. Learn from them and give over to others the ones you find valuable.

"Before I say goodbye, Bella, I would like to share three final thoughts with you." Bella pretended to ignore Cee, acting as if she hadn't said anything.

"Please listen carefully, Bella. I would like you to promise me you will do the first insight always, the second almost always, and the third, never.

"First: Believe in life, Bella—Always. Life is overwhelmingly good. It is overwhelmingly kind and generous. Be thrilled about what life has given to you and confident about what it has in store for you.

"Next: Smile—Almost always. Happiness is the starting point and the facilitator of everything a creature does. A sense of joyfulness and the ability to project a powerful and engaging smile will energize you and all of those around you. There will be tears in life, but try to smile through your tears whenever you can.

"Finally: Retire—Never. If you ever think of kicking up your trunk and taking it easy—think again. Never stop challenging life in each of the key areas: career, learning, and giving to others. Life is about living; not retiring. Never stop expressing your uniqueness. Never stop revealing your excellence and chasing it—whatever it is and wherever it takes you. Live fully and intensely—until you die."

And with that, Cee smiled and, with a flutter of his left wing, he was gone.

As Bella sat at her desk, somewhat in shock, in through the office door barged one of the handsomest male elephants she had ever seen. And behind him, a serious-looking large, green turtle.

To be continued . . .

Jungle Parables

Parables have been passed down from generation to generation for thousands of years. Small and large communal gatherings were built around an uplifting parable presented by a sage or respected leader. Listeners would step away inspired and emboldened—possessing new insights for success. Parables remain a rich and cherished part of all cultures—as relevant today as when they were first written.

THE FIRST STEP TO SUCCESS

The World Was Created for Me!

My dear child,

The World Was Created for You!

Each morning, wake up, smile, stand tall, and stretch your arms as high as you can, and say,

"The World Was Created for Me!"

Think about the huge mountains with peaks that reach to the heavens, and say,

"Those beautiful mountains with the peaks that are so tall, were created for me!"

Picture quiet streams and strong, thunderous rivers, and say,

"The trickling water and the powerful current were made for me!"

Look at the discoveries all around you that make the world so small and its possibilities so remarkable, and say,

"Every idea that became real is a gift to me!"

Wonder about the unsolved mysteries of the heavens and the earth, the deep oceans, and our own bodies, and say,

"It's all there, the simple and complex, the obvious and mysterious— waiting for me!"

Smile at the beings in your world, the thinkers and dreamers, the mighty and the meek, and say,

"They are all here, each one unique yet connected; all brought together for me!"

The World Was Created for Me!

And then, close your eyes for a moment and

climb the mountains, from end to end

Walk to the top of the peaks, through the clouds, so that you touch the
> *heavens*
Run quickly into the stream
Swim mightily across the rivers
Come up with a new invention
and give it a name
Be inspired by the questions you will someday answer
> *and by all of the creatures in your life*
It's all here just for you!
The World Was Created for You!
Each day, as you dream and grow,
as you begin to build, design, and discover, climb and touch, invent and
> *ask . . .*
Know that you help create the world for those around you
so that all children (and adults) will wake up each morning, smile,
> *stand tall, and stretch their arms as high as they can and say:*
The World Was Created for Me!

SEARCHING TO FIND ONESELF

The Longest Short Road

*The hopeful young pup, childlike in his optimism, left home to find his
    dream*

He traversed great mountains of thought

Swam expansive rivers of theory

Tiptoed through fields of ancient wisdom

Tasted the fruits of spirituality of many lands and different beings

And he traveled far from home.

The most revered of scholarship

The most sensitizing of spirituality

Profound possibilities of knowledge

Loneliness growing daily as the real questions remained unanswerable.

After many years and just a few minutes

his heart was somewhat defeated

and his search was over.

His plan: To infuse joy into his reality, and redefine his reality as his dream.

His belief: The search was for naught

He had traveled so far from home.

How sad and uplifting

*His dream was on his lips, by his fingertips, in his heart, and through
    his spirit.*

He must traverse the greatest mountain,

the mountain of the acceptance of his uniqueness.

He must swim the most expansive river,

the river of the affirmation of his greatness.

May he allow his lips to speak courageously, his fingertips to touch
deeply, his heart to soar rather than simply be.
The most revered of scholarship
The most sensitizing of spirituality
Profound possibilities of knowledge
Loneliness disappearing as he discovered himself.
And he and his dream were one
and lived happily together forever

THE HONESTY TO SUCCEED

The Three Angels

The Angels of Love, Honesty, and Death came together for an
important meeting at the top of a tall mountain.
Their task: To determine who had the most difficult job.
The Angel of Death spoke first and said,
"My mission is the toughest of all,
in that living creatures have yet to
understand that I am a friend, not a foe;
a blessing, not a curse; a beginning, not an end.
I am a partner in the process of creation and the quest for happiness."
The Angel of Love spoke next,
"My mission is certainly the most difficult.
Creatures are afraid to work hard, as hard as they must,
so I may live between them,
so I may live within them."
After much thought, the Angel of Honesty spoke in a low voice with
carefully chosen words interrupted by tears.
And he said, "I am a creature's future;
I am its past. I am its ability to see,
to hear, to cry, to smile.
I am its ability to love.
I am its understanding of death, in that only through me may it
experience life."
They nodded to each other approvingly, and were gone.

Risk Taking

The River

I'm hungry
> *Cross the river*

I'm afraid
> *Your failure could never be as great as your fear*
>> *Cross the river*

Life has forsaken me
> *It brought you to the river*
>> *Cross the river*

Do others understand?
> *Understanding need not be anyone's but yours*
>> *Cross the river*

I'm confused
> *You're hungry*
>> *Cross the river*

I can't swim
> *The depth of the river is determined by your belief*
>> *Cross the river*

It's dark
> *You are the creator of your darkness*
>> *Cross the river*

Maybe tomorrow
> *Tomorrow will bring another river*
>> *Cross the river*

FAILURE IS A LIBERATOR

Life's Magic Potion

I fell and fell, deeper and deeper.

*Finally, I stopped falling, and I simply closed my eyes and slept for
decades and a moment.*

How funny, nothing to feel, nothing to see, no one around me.

How crazy; I am not frightened, I am not sad.

I am surprised;

it seems I am fine.

I am light; I am free.

How wonderful; no yesterday, no today, no tomorrow.

I have fallen, I am free.

How wonderful; no you, no her, no me.

I have fallen, I am free.

*I have become one with the trees and the rivers, and the ground and the
sky and the heavens.*

How wonderful; I have fallen, I am free.

I can never be frightened again.

And now, real choices,

to be introduced to freedom amidst great loss—the loss of the fear to live.

Everyone should fall at least once in this lifetime!

A Greater Good

The Little Me

*There is an opinion in ancient text that says every act of mine creates
a living being of the expression of that act in the world of the
nonphysical.*

Every beautiful thing I do,

creates a beautiful little me

who will live forever as the embodiment of that act.

Every less than beautiful thing I do,

creates a less than beautiful little me

who will live forever as the embodiment of that act.

*Over time, hundreds and thousands of these little beings will be running
around in this reflective world (where there are no limitations of
the physical and everything is forever),*

*expressing who they are in the ultimate sense, in that all they can ever be
is exactly what they were created as.*

*At the end of my days, this opinion states, I will not be judged by
another, but simply by the little eternal expressions of me which
I created.*

*If the beautiful little beings are the majority, the scales will be tipped to
their advantage. And if the less than beautiful little beings are in
the majority, then the scales of my ultimate destiny will be tipped
to their advantage.*

*It is a wonderful perspective in that it affirms: I create my destiny
today, tomorrow, forever.*

How are your little ones doing?

LIVING YOUR CAREER DREAM

Real Fun

Hearts starting to beat softly with the hint of excitement, and the
beginning of a smile, driven by a purpose, by a plan
Minds shining with a new energy
and the laughter of a childlike adventure to a candy store of growth
candies
Ideas crowding and pushing at your consciousness each eager to get a
hearing
There is a liberation grabbed on to daily.
To have the courage to dream—
the unrealistic, the illogical,
the nondefendable horizons of joy
that no one may promise or guarantee.
And to then couple that dream
with a plan to bring it to life
And to then live a piece of that dream
every day in thought, in word, and in action.
You touch it, you feel it, you hold it,
it touches you, it lifts you.
Less important things disappear from your thoughts—there is no time or
place for them
Energies that are not for building are pushed aside
There is a skip in your walk, a mystery about your presence
Others will want to be near you, to be part of what you care about
There is a different purpose as you begin your mornings
Your time is precious and carefully measured

Your days are quick, full, energizing,
building blocks to a true legacy.
To have the courage to dream
the unrealistic, the illogical,
the nondefendable horizons of joy
that no one may promise or guarantee
The confidence to couple that dream
with a plan to bring it to life
And the will to live a piece of that dream every day
in thoughts, words, and actions

To Believe in Life

Love of Life

Your clouds stand at attention, with great pride, manning the gates of the vast horizon.

Your waters sparkle and move, yet are remarkably silent. Their silence is rich and vivid, yet still and humbling.

Your eagles stand alone, each one as a spirit of what might be, a spirit of what is, and a guardian of the moment.

Your air is so rich I can taste it and its taste fills me.

Your harvest, the wheat and barley, the grapes and olives, stand quietly—seeing it all as part of it all.

Small birds charge across your vistas, powerful and determined in their purpose and direction. More birds—large and small—fly as a group and fly as one.

Your skies smile warmly, offering layers of great insight wrapped in remarkable beauty.

The color of your endless seas touches the color of your vast horizon, creating new color, becoming hues of blue and hues of pink.

The mandate: Fly low to the ground yet touch the outermost horizon!

Live in this world of the clouds and the waters, the eagles and the air, the harvest, the birds, and the skies—and the color touching color to create new color.

Grab hold of the heavens, revel in the silence, feel the spirit of the past, present, and future in each moment, taste the air and allow it to flow through you.

We will fly low to the ground yet touch the outermost horizon.

Dear life, You have empowered us!

The Book of Cee

A well-traveled butterfly gleans invaluable ideas as she journeys from place to place, experiencing, learning, and growing. There is no better teacher than a life lived.

Self-Love

- Smile quickly and often. Smile at yourself first.
- Laugh quickly and often. Laugh at yourself first.
- Learn a new joke every day.
- Praise quickly and often. Praise yourself first.
- To make the same mistake a few times is expected.
- Forgive quickly and often. Forgive yourself first.
- Lethargy and laziness are the un-doings of a living being. The unwillingness to act due to either of those inclinations will have far-reaching consequences.
- Attempt to identify and eradicate lethargy with a call-to-action mindset.
- The ability of something to break beyond repair is one of the most effective enablers of life. Endings create life.

- There is no word in ancient languages for vacation.
- If you're doing what your love, why vacate the effort? Commit more and vacate less.
- There is no word in ancient languages for "retire." Retirement is an antilife concept that should be vacated completely.
- Those whom have risked their lives for an idea or another creature live in a reality that is richer, greater, and more fulfilling than the one all others live in.
- Questions are life's learning tool. Be comfortable with more questions than answers. Teach those around you to consider answers but to cherish questions.
- Learn a new word every day.
- Learn about a new part of your body every week.
- Learn the name of the capital of a country every month.

Building Character and Fineness

- Every being should have a musical expression. Some should compose, others should produce, some should play the oboe and others the drums. Indulge your music expression even if it is limited. Your music expression will make you more complete, more fulfilled, and more successful.
- Every being should have an artistic expression. Some should sculpt, others should carve, some should use metals, and others stone. Attempt an art expression. It will make you more complete, more stimulated.

- Stand up when your mother or father walk into the room. Stand regardless of whom has achieved more success or whom has a more respected position in the community.

- Stand up when someone older or wiser enters the room. Age and wisdom engender respect. Respecting others habitually enshrines good character.

- Never sit in your mother or father's seat without his/her permission.

- Never call a parent by his/her first name. The terms "Mom" or "Dad" denote the same expression of respect as Dr. or Judge. Proper respect through use of titles is extremely important regarding those closest to us.

- Never feel entitled to anything. Never feel like you "deserve" something or "you've earned it." Whenever you see yourself thinking, saying, or being told those words, it probably means you're reaching for something you can either live without or shouldn't have.

- Speak slowly and softly. Use words that are pretty and fine.

- Any word can be made into a four-letter word. It's all about how you say something.

- If you're a father you have a different vocabulary than your son. If you're a grandfather you have a different vocabulary than your father. If you're a business leader you have a different vocabulary than your employee. Words must be appropriate to a creature's station. Words that are okay for him may not be okay for you.

- Sticks and stones may break your bones. Hurtful words will break your spirit. Words are more powerful than stones.

- Respect and love for others are not simply duties of the heart. They are actionable, requiring goals, a plan, checks and balances.

- There is no more exalted profession than teaching. There is no greater gift you can give a person than the tools to learn.

- Make an effort to teach the skills you've acquired while building your career.

- Learn the name and a single composition of one classic musician each month. It will make you a more interesting and sought after being.

- Rebuke those you can impact; never judge anyone. Rebuking brings about growth and an important confrontation with reality. Judging others brings about anger, the belittling of others, and ultimately the belittling of self.

- If you judge others, you will be subject to judgment. The more harshly you judge, the more harshly you will be judged.

- The lack of rebuke will bring about the decay of society.

- The thief steals an amount for which he can be jailed. The fiend steals less than that which he can be held accountable. The fiend is much more dangerous than the thief.

- A wonderful family custom is to sit together one night each week describing an outstanding act of kindness each has done. Mom and Dad should start. Helping an old elephant across the stream is nice, but not outstanding. Over time you will find that your children don't have one outstanding act of kindness to report, but several.

- A wonderful dinner custom is to go around each night and share a new idea or insight you've learned. With that you will build a love of knowledge in your children.

- The best family custom of all is to go around and each one tell a joke. It should start with the most serious animal. Humor is an expression of love and one of life's cherished elements.

- The foundation of every relationship is trust. Trust means I can give over my most fragile, easily trampled upon fears, hopes, and concerns to you and you will never hurt me with them.

- Live your life as if there were a camera focused on everything you do and say—with a direct feed to those whom you love and respect most.

- It's important to be very articulate about the kindness you do for others. Your children will learn from your actions only if they hear again and again about your actions.

- When it comes to creatures we love, it's more about peace and keeping a being emotionally whole than it is about truth.

- Don't say what's on your mind. Use your mind to carefully edit and measure what you say.

- There is no greater expression of strength than silence.

- Train yourself. Being shrewd is better than being smart. Being shrewd means sometimes letting the other guy win. Small defeats enable big victories.

- As a member of the animal kingdom you are responsible for the well-being of those you have the ability to help; even if you have to reach further than you've reached before to exercise that help.

- Be a student of all whom you love. Make an ongoing effort to learn everything about your lifelong partner, your parents, and each of your children. Keep in mind the fact that nothing and no one stands still. The one you are engaging today is different than the one you engaged a week ago.

- Assuming you helped two beings, giving one several hours of your time after he'd been suffering for several days and the other one immediate help that took only a few hours of your time. In the grand scheme of things, your help to the second being is greater in that your immediate response enabled less of him to shatter.

- When a creature shatters emotionally, there will invariably be a piece of him that cannot be repaired and dies.

- In the collective equation of existence there is no such status as neutral.

- In the individual equation there is no such status as neutral. You are either growing intellectually, emotionally, spiritually, and practically, or you are receding. There is no standing still.
- Live long and happy—each day.

About the Author

Ricky Cohen is a successful businessman and a perpetual entrepreneur. After graduating Cum Laude from New York University, Cohen quickly assumed the leadership role in what was then a small family business. By successfully combining the tools he learned in the classroom with wisdom dating back thousands of years and his strong penchant for risk taking, Cohen grew *Conway Stores* fortyfold in sales and profits in less than a decade. His success was a result of the emphasis he placed on risk taking and personal leadership: every employee in the Conway organization was infused with an entrepreneurial spirit and the tools to achieve on unprecedented levels.

Cohen is a dynamic and exciting speaker and motivator. Over the last three decades, Cohen has educated thousands of entrepreneurs and intra-preneurs—empowering the will, inspiring the mind, and providing the skills needed for individual and corporate, immediate and long-term success. "Every Employee an Entrepreneur" is an incredibly powerful workshop that industry leaders have implemented in their companies, inspiring dramatic, quantifiable growth in individuals and the organization.

Tens of thousands look to Cohen for guidance in all areas of life, from love and relationships to moral and ethical dilemmas. His rubric includes books and articles in all the categories and weekly workshops in the New York Metropolitan area.

Cohen is currently Chairman and CEO of The Conway Organization and serves in a leadership role on several community and educational not-for-profit organizations. Cohen lives in Brooklyn, New York, with his wife Jamie and their children.

For more information on Ricky, to schedule a workshop, and to stay up to date with his new releases, visit www.rickycohen.org.